THE HEART FLAME

written and illustrated
by

Christine McBride

No part of the publication may be reproduced, stored in a retrieval system, or transmitted in any form or by any means, electronic, mechanical, photocopying, recording, or otherwise, without written permission of the author/creator. For information regarding persmission write to
theheartflame1@gmail.com
www.theheartflame.com

For

Simone Dylan

whose light shines so bright,
my world it does light.

with love, Mimi

It matters not how small how tall,
there is a flame within us all.

It makes its home within your heart,
mindfulness will be your part.

Our flame can travel tip to toes,
but heart is where it's fed and grows.

It can grow bright it can grow dim,
you choose the size of your flame within.

"How?" you ask, "Do I control the flame?
I'm just a kid, I only know my name!"

Well just like fire needs wood to burn,
our flame burns thoughts at every turn!

Good thoughts keep it burning bright,
thoughts of love and you'll feel light.

Bad thoughts cause it to diminish,
Fearful thoughts and you'll feel squeamish.

Dwell too long on thoughts that scare you,
flame becomes too small to warm you.

It will slip from its home in your happy heart,
all the way down with a bump in the dark.

Below it'll stay, twisting, turning,
the only thoughts here are fear for burning.

The gnawing, the chewing, the hollowing out,
with feelings so big you scream and shout!

The worrying, fretting and wringing your hands,
are signs your heart flame is not in command.

But lucky for you there's a simple solution,
to wipe from your mind all the stinky pollution.

Keep your light fed, keep it safe and secure,
happy at home in your heart is the cure.

Allowing yourself to feel love is the best,
for making flame feel at home in its nest.

Alone in your room hold your heart with your hands,
then whisper the words only it understands.

Begin with the words I love who I am,
I'm happy and whole so fear you can scram!

I am light, I am love, I'm kindness and joy,
I'm song, I'm dance, I'm happiness ahoy!

I'm strong, I'm smart, I'm caring and calm,
knowing I'm enough keeps me happy all day long!

Now just take a moment to feel all the love,
your flame gives you back with its heat from above.

The love you invest to keep your flame safe,
is the love it gives back tenfold in its place.

Thoughts that you swell on, tell on and dwell on,
are thoughts your heart seeds on, needs on and feeds on.

So keep your flame up from out of the deep,
think thoughts filled with love and with joy before sleep.

Thoughts before bed set the tone for tomorrow,
you don't want your day filled with grief or with sorrow.

So take time today, right now, straight away!
Don't wait one more minute, or hour, or day!

To fill up your mind with wondrous notions,
so good dreams will come, like magical potions.

When counting your blessings your light grows so bright,
so big and so wondrous the world it does light.

For miles ahead it'll light up your way,
cherish your flame and long it'll stay.

Your light will shine on filling days with its songs
and you'll feel the love when it's where it belongs!

The secret that most have yet to uncover,
is thoughts of self love FEEL so good. You'll discover.

Don't ever let anyone make you feel shame,
for you are the powerful, the unconquerable heart flame!

About the author/illustrator

Christine McBride

Artist, writer, yoga instructor, empath and Reiki practioner, Christine has moved through her own personal challenges of a disabling accident, cancer, autoimmune disease, depression and PTSD. She uses movement, mindfulness (MRT), breath, art and writing to help recondition the body's response to trauma and stress. Whether in the past or present day, moving through a crisis into your own awakening is possible. She uses her creativity to help others learn how to let go and love themselves.

A full life is waiting for you on the other side of ptsd, anxiety/depression and illness. You just have to be fearless moving into it.

Made in the USA
Las Vegas, NV
13 February 2024